YOU ARE ONLY JUST BEGINNING

LESSONS FOR THE JOURNEY AHEAD

MORGAN HARPER NICHOLS

 ZONDERVAN®

Zondervan

You Are Only Just Beginning

© 2023 Morgan Harper Nichols

Requests for information should be addressed to:
Zondervan, *3900 Sparks Dr. SE, Grand Rapids, Michigan 49546*

ISBN 978-0-31046-076-3 (audiobook)
ISBN 978-0-31046-075-6 (eBook)
ISBN 978-0-31046-074-9 (HC)

Any internet addresses (websites, blogs, etc.) and telephone numbers in this book are offered as a resource. They are not intended in any way to be or imply an endorsement by Zondervan, nor does Zondervan vouch for the content of these sites and numbers for the life of this book.

Art direction: Tiffany Forrester
Interior design: Mallory Collins and Morgan Harper Nichols

Printed in the United States of America

23 24 25 26 27 VER 6 5 4 3 2

TABLE OF CONTENTS

INTRODUCTION

There's a wooden train track that runs through my living room, into the kitchen, and toward the front door. This train is unlike any other, some cars carrying freight, while others house passengers with passports from all corners of the earth. It's an international railroad system engineered and run by my little boy, Jacob. I am mostly an outside observer, but there is much to be explored in the world he has created with this train weaving through my home. So many stories of adventure to tell, and I want to hear them all. He's two, so the stories aren't that well-formed yet. He's only just beginning to play, to dream. But I never know what he's going to come up with, and I'm always pleasantly surprised. I know it's going to be good, if he's the one writing the story.

As the co-conductor of my own life, I want to live my life with my son's sense of hope and curiosity for the future. No matter if you're two, thirty-two, or one hundred and two, you are only just beginning, always on the brink of discovering something new. While you can't always determine the path you'll take in this life, you do have the choice to set out every day with hope and agency to make goodness your future.

Trust me, I know the future can be frightening. It's all unknown. But I want us to learn to embrace the miracle of moving forward—to plan ahead and dream of what goodness could be. To choose to be present in each chapter of the journey—yes, even the difficult moments. Because there is so much to be learned from every new adventure, even the parts we'd rather forget.

This book is my poetic take on the heroine's journey, from the call to adventure all the way to journeying back home. For every stage of adventure, I look to an organism, object, or ecosystem for inspiration. There are lessons to be learned from all of these, and as I set out on new adventures, I find it calming to observe the world all around me. This practice of curiosity makes me feel like I'm part of something bigger, to know the whole world is constantly changing and moving and learning, too. All of us, together, in forward motion.

My hope is that this book can be an invitation to embrace curiosity as you take your next step into your future. I can't tell you what lies ahead, but I can tell you this: As long as you are breathing, there is more to your story. Wherever you may be as you hold this book in your hands, I invite you to join me on my personal journey of encouraging your imagination to overflow with good. And when you do, I believe you'll discover Grace is woven throughout the everyday. We simply need to train our eyes and hearts to see it.

I cannot tell you
what lies ahead
but I can tell you:
As long as you are breathing,
you are only just beginning.

MHN

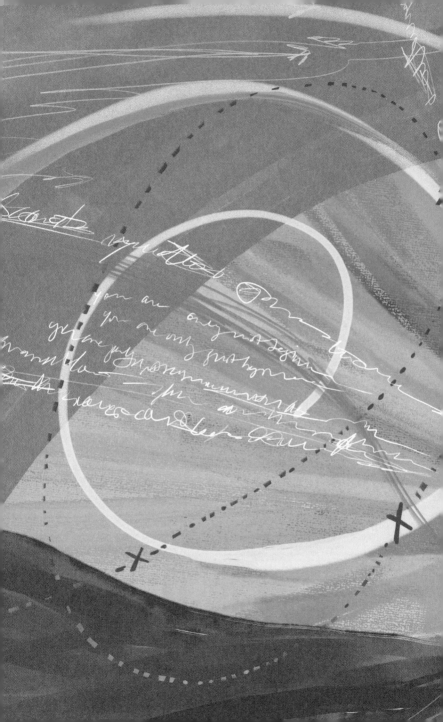

BEGINNING A NEW ADVENTURE

LESSONS FROM SUNLIGHT

WHAT WE LEARN FROM SUNLIGHT

Every morning the sun rises, and every single day, the sun's rays take us on a journey. Hour by hour, as light moves across the sky, we experience the world in new color and shadow, until the sun finally sets, only to start its journey again the following morning. Day by day, the sun brings forth new life. Even if it's just gentle sunrays pouring in through the nearest window, we know sunlight makes a difference in our lives.

And with every sunrise, we are reminded that as long as we are here, under these glorious golden rays, there is more to our stories. Another day is dawning, and with every new morning, we are invited to step out into our futures with a sense of hope and adventure.

So whenever you feel the heat of the sun's beams or notice her light dancing through trees, may you remember this radiant truth—there is more to your story. There is more for you just up ahead. And no matter how much you've already seen in this life, Light will continue to show up for you every day. Dare to keep your heart open.

Let every beam of sunlight be a fresh reminder of this calling: New adventure awaits you.

WHENEVER I AM WORRIED
I WON'T HAVE ENOUGH ENERGY,
I SLOWLY LIFT MY CHIN
AND FIX MY TIRED EYES
JUST BEYOND THE
HALF-CLOSED MORNING BLINDS
WHERE I AM REMINDED
THAT IF THE SUNRISE
CAN EASE INTO A NEW DAY,
THEN SO CAN I.

JUST AS THE SUN,
A NEW DAY CALLS MY NAME.
AND I AM FREE
TO SLOWLY RISE INTO IT ALL THE SAME.

IF THE SUN RISES SLOWLY
INTO THE DAY, THEN SO CAN I.
IF THE SUN RISES SLOWLY
INTO THE DAY, THEN SO CAN I.

3

There are some days
adventure calls me
in the form of a bright yellow rotary phone
hanging on the kitchen wall.
I rush to answer and I twirl my fingers
through the curly plastic cord
and say,
"Yes!"
I take the trip.
I take the leap.
I breathe deep and leave home,
to go and do a brave new thing.

But most days,
adventure calls in the form
of a secret whisper
floating into my ear
and asking,
"What's next?"
Adventure calls me
to notice the wonder right here
in all that I have deemed insignificant.

When adventure calls
as a whisper
and not as a yellow rotary phone,
I'm reminded that the start of a new adventure
can also take place at home.

I trace the shadows shifting
as they slog across the room.
Pushed by sunlight,
day after day,
they're constantly moving.

Just like sunlight,
I notice the shadows are on their own journey, too.

I don't need a time lapse to watch them closely.
I don't need a compass to see where they can go.
Today, sunlight is a friend of shadows,
whispers
of adventure,
at home.

WHEN IT COMES
TO NEW BEGINNINGS
~~PUSH YOURSELF~~
PACE YOURSELF
SHINE LIKE THE SUN DOES
TAKING YOUR TIME TO RISE

You cannot hold sunlight
in your hands
but you know it
by every living plant,
creature,
life
it affects.

You know it
by the way
the pothos stretches its leaves,
inching and eking
to become the light's friend.

You know it
by the way
it summons your cat
to bask in the light,
hypnotizing her in heat
for an afternoon nap.

You know it
by the way it sings to you
through the window
after the longest nights:
"Today is a new day
and here, there is room
to shine bright,
unapologetically,
like gold,
how you were
always meant to."

Right now is the moment.

Every particle of light within you knows it's true.

Take your time to get used to the changes.
There is no need to rush
as you're ushered into light.
Listen to your body
as you adjust to a new phase of your life.
Don't feel pressured
to figure out everything right away.

Even in these unknowns,
starting over can start slowly.
You do not need to rush.
You will gather new rhythms as you go.

Adventure is the blank page of a passport,
the camera battery fully charged,
the travel itinerary scheduled to the brim,
the train rides over country lines,
the new recipe you're daring to try,
the curiosity in a child's eyes,
the opening of a new book for the first time,
the album you've been waiting for,
the excitement of the unknown,
the awakening feeling of learning to fly
beyond the bounds of your comfort zone.

Here's to embracing
the call of adventure.
Here's to crossing the threshold
of what you've called home
of all you have ever known
in exchange
for tomorrow.

Here's to accepting that your fears
might catch up to you
but remembering your courage
will catch up, too.
Now is the time to allow yourself
to be shaped by the new.

Take your first steps
toward the mountain
your soul
has been calling you to climb.
The winds of doubt
blow fast around you.
You have to learn to breathe again
at the higher altitudes.
The terrain
makes you question the strength
of your spine, lungs, and heart.
But you will come down
the other side realizing
you are stronger
than you thought you were.

THE SUN'S
GOLDEN FINGERS
REACH OUT TO ME.
I CAN FEEL THEM ON MY SKIN.
AND I WELCOME
          MUCH-NEEDED
             WARMTH
                FOR MY
             TIRED SOUL.
           WARMTH
      SPILLING OUT IN A
      BILLION TINY SUNRAYS.
         MY HEART STARTS
    TO POUND MORE HEAVILY
      FOR RIGHT HERE,
         AT DAWN.
    HOPE HAS STIRRED ME.
       I MUST GO.

Am I really doing this?
Am I going to leave all I've ever known?

I have to go.

I can see what's behind me
in the distance.
I am scared.
This is going to take a lot of me
to step forward and to go.

I've never seen this done before.
I don't know what my future has in store.
I hold my breath, fearing that it will betray
all the fear I have inside,
how much I just want to stay.

But the only way to go is forward.
I promise
I'll come back someday,
but for now
I'm headed northward.

I WILL NOT WAIT FOR THE PERFECT DAY. I WILL NOT WAIT FOR THE PERFECT TIME. TODAY IS THE DAY, THE MINUTE, AND THE PLACE I CHOOSE TO LIVE.

It's too late to turn back.
A new day is coming.

I am
accepting the wrinkles
that come through the years
and the laugh lines, too.

I am
remembering the days
we shared mornings together
over warm coffee
and rock-hard biscotti
dreaming out loud of what
adventures we might take.

I've lost track
of the Sunshine State key chain.
I kept forgetting
to attach it to the key ring.
I've lost track
of our good intentions
and all our half-finished plans.

I carry our memories,
a little lighter now.

I take my first step
toward a new me,
a new day.
And another and another
into the next crossway.
My heart breaks,
but grace
leads the way.
I'm afraid to start this journey,
but I go anyway.

I'd do anything to go back,
but we were made to travel onward.

WHAT ARE YOU TELLING YOURSELF
THAT MIGHT NOT BE THE TRUTH?
WHAT WORRIES HAVE HELD YOU BACK
THAT ARE WORTH LEARNING
HOW TO PUSH THROUGH?

You're finally doing it.
You're finally here.
You've been talking
about scouring for flights,
packing your bags,
and now,
as you grip your
passport in your hand,
breathe in the chilled air,
and take your first
crunchy step in the day-old snow,
your dreams are
no longer just dreams.
They're true.
You can smell them in the pine.
You can taste them in the salty air.
And every sensation is
an invitation
to climb higher and higher.
The future is now.

8 SIGNS YOU'RE READY FOR AN ADVENTURE OF DISCOVERY

1

The prospect of discovering what that looks like excites you more than it scares you.

2

You're beginning to surround yourself with people who share in your joy of using your childlike imagination to foster hope in the now and the future.

3

You're open to taking unexpected turns, and you're ready to learn.

4

You're starting to embrace that everyone is at different points of the circular journey of life, and you are worth no less if you are in a different place than someone you look up to.

5

You recognize there are parts of life that are out of your control, and your fear of not being good enough won't stop you from carrying on.

6

You're learning how to work through fear one breath at a time.

7

You're starting to be less afraid of trying new things. You are becoming less attached to worrying about what the outcome will be.

8

You're becoming open to the idea that even though you feel stuck where you are at times, as sure as the sun continues to rise and set, you are free to wake up to life. You are starting to find joy in ordinary days. You are learning to travel onward by pacing yourself on a path that is flooded with gloriously radiant Light.

FINDING YOUR PEOPLE

LESSONS FROM ELEPHANTS

WHAT WE LEARN FROM ELEPHANTS

Elephants are deeply intelligent and relational creatures. They soothe their crying babies and hold funerals for the deceased. They play and fight and reconcile. They are present to themselves and each other. That's real community—caring for one another. Each herd is led by a single matriarch, to whom the rest of the herd looks for wisdom. They rely on one another for protection and never travel alone—always traveling as a true herd.

As I step out in a new adventure, I often find myself asking, *Who is in my herd?* I'm constantly connected on social media, and I'm always meeting more and more new and wonderful people. It's easier than ever to build a wide network. I'm c*onnected* more than ever before, yet somehow it's easy to feel like I'm not really *connecting*.

Just like elephants, you and I were made for connection. We're fundamentally wired to need other people. What a beautiful truth—to need one another. But finding your people can also feel like an overwhelming struggle. Let me encourage you that "finding your people" does not always have to mean adding new people to your life. It's likely that the people you need for the next step of your journey are already present in your life. We simply need to embrace the slow and steady practice of cultivating deep and meaningful relationships, rather than more of them. Because these are the relationships we need to step into our futures.

Let's let these gorgeous creatures remind us that we need one another for the journey ahead.

Elephants
trumpet and roar
to one another in secret codes,
like children on a playground
yelling to one another
in languages only kids can understand.

One waves his trunk
like a child waving wildly on the field,
pleading *I'm open.*
Choose me.
Can I be part of your team?

At the end of the day
their rumbling turns to rustling,
and they settle into silence.

At least that's how it seems.
But I've watched long enough to know
that just because I don't understand
their rhythms and sounds
doesn't mean
nothing is being said.
Perhaps
there is much for us to learn
from the space between the sounds
if we dare to slow down
and listen.

As I watched the elephants,
I marveled at the quiet.

I watched them settle down together
as the sun began to set.

I yearn for a bond like that.
The gift of family.
Tell me, what could be better?

The dark dome of night
descends on the savanna,
and a blanket of stars cloaks the sky above.

In the quiet,
I sense a collective confidence . . .
everyone knows they will be alright.
They look out for each other.
No one will be left alone.

This is what we were made for.
I pray it's not a dream.
I hold on to this memory,
fearful that it will escape into the recesses
of where the good memories go
and that I'll wake up
alone.

The journey back to the village
feels twice as long,
as I sigh
and hope
that what I saw
may be possible for me, too.

Will I ever know a love like this?

I am starting to believe
under this savanna light
with a small twinkle in my eye
it's possible.
Even though
that hope feels faint,
I tuck it away.
I commit to slowly
walk with grace.

Be present with others
however you can
    through your words
    your time
    your passions
whatever it is you bring,
do your best,
open your ears,
and stand for one another.

YOU MAY
NEVER KNOW
HOW THE PATH
YOU TREAD
MADE WAY
FOR OTHERS

27

NOTES ON
BEING A
GOOD FRIEND:
LISTEN WELL.
GIVE TIME.
INVOLVE THE HEART
WHEN YOU ARE ASKED
FOR ADVICE.
LAUGH WITH THOSE
WHO LAUGH.
WEEP WITH THOSE WHO WEEP.
SHOW GRATITUDE
FOR EVERY LITTLE
MOMENT YOU HAVE TO
MAKE SOMEONE
ELSE FEEL SEEN.

OVER TIME,
COMMUNITY
WILL CHANGE.
SOMEONE
WILL MOVE.
DISTANCE
WILL GROW.

SOMETIMES
IT ACHES
TO LET OUR
PRESENT BECOME
OUR PAST.

HOLD SPACE
FOR THE BEAUTY
OF WHAT WAS
AND STILL IS.
PLEASE.
TRUST.
THERE IS
MORE TO COME.

Like the whipping wind
of an open desert storm,
your emotions mix
and clash
and you feel like you will never rest again
until you can settle
your score.

As you try to make sense of all
that was misunderstood and left unsaid,
as you try to keep your balance
on an uncharted path,
you'll go back and forth wondering
who was in the wrong
and whether these relationships can withstand
these heavy winds blowing cold, ever increasing.

Hidden in the dunes,
you wonder if an apology
will abate the rage,
but somehow you can't say it yet.
Not yet.
Not you.
Why should you?

You wait and you wait.
Silently.
You cover your eyes.
Fight against the pressure
of the wind.
You know you can't hide here forever.

So you step out
and step again
until you reach the pool of water
where you've been before.
You see your face in the glass.
You see your reflection and remember who you are.

And look up.

And see your face in their faces, too.

You hear the hollowness
of nothing
as the dust settles.
The winds have slowed down
and in the silence you sit and ask
an honest question of one another:
Are we really that different after all?

Sometimes we must
take action
to show our compassion.

And sometimes,
the best thing we can do
is be a loving presence,
with no words at all.
Perhaps all they need
in this moment
is to not be alone.

LONELINESS
IS AN ENDLESS ECHO
OF YOURSELF.

TAKE HEART,
OPEN YOUR EARS
AND LISTEN.
LOVE IS CALLING.

May we always look
out for one another.
May we always be willing to go
the extra mile in search of water,
not only for ourselves
but for the sake of the other.
May we never forget
we were made to be in community,
never made to do this life alone.
Your small act of being present
will go a long way.
May we only continue to grow
and learn from each other.
As elephants living together
learn from one another,
let's embrace the wisdom
of those who came before us.
Let us hold dear
all of the notes of survival
that have been passed down
and shared among us.
May we never forget
that the greatest gift
we have to give to another
is love.

When life's desert winds pick up
and you are left alone in a cloud of dust,
trust that your pack is there.
Even as the world swirls around you,
reach out,
hold on,
tightly—
you don't have to go alone.

I cannot tell you when
the days will become clear.
But you have a choice
how you will move forward.
The steps you take,
the pace you race.
Go slow, go fast.
But remember to reach out to one another
in the form of phone conversations
or hand-written letters
You can always find strength
in the strength of your herd.

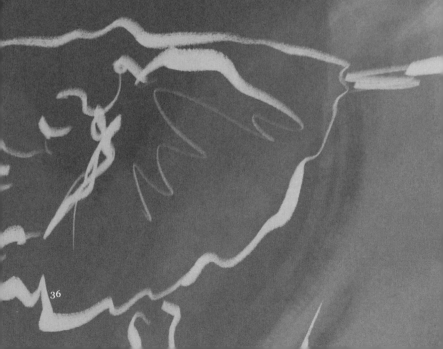

GRANDMOTHER ELEPHANT
HELPS
THE YOUNG SURVIVE.
GRANDMOTHER ELEPHANT
KNOWS THE WAY
TO WATER,
TO FOOD,
WHAT EVERYONE NEEDS FOR LIFE.

LET HER LIFE STORY
BE YOUR GUIDE.
DO NOT LET HER WISDOM PASS YOU BY.

Whenever you feel lost
and unsure of the path before you
because you are still trying to make sense
of all the steps behind you,
look down to the ground beneath your feet.
You will find there is a path.
It is not paved, but there are tracks—
weighted and considerate—
Mother Elephant knew the way.
One step at a time you can follow her steps.
She knew you would be here today.

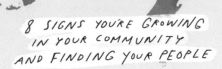

8 SIGNS YOU'RE GROWING IN YOUR COMMUNITY AND FINDING YOUR PEOPLE

1

You're becoming more curious
about the people who are already in your life.

2

You are no longer comparing your community to others.

3

You are open to meeting new people, but you're not
pressuring yourself.

4

You're learning that time spent together
in silence is still time well spent.

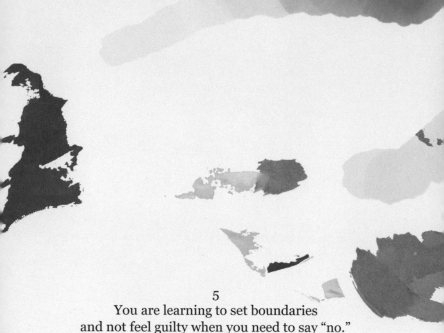

5
You are learning to set boundaries
and not feel guilty when you need to say "no."

6
You're recognizing the power of quality over quantity
when it comes to the closest relationships in your life.

7
You're learning what it looks like to take care
of one another.

8
You're looking for opportunities
to serve those you love.

GOING DEEPER

LESSONS FROM THE OCEAN

WHAT WE LEARN FROM
THE OCEAN AND ITS CURRENTS

For most of us, it's nearly impossible to judge the ocean's depths. It has strong currents, unpredictable to the average adventurer, and it can be dangerous to dive deep without knowledge and skill. And yet, some of the most wondrous sights on this earth are held in its water. We instinctively want to know more about what's underneath the water's surface. We can read about it, but for those who actually dive deep and observe the beauty and wonder under the surface, the experience can be life-changing. Despite the risks of deep-sea diving, there's a reason these explorers keep going back below the upper layers of the current. There's something intangible to be learned in the depths of the ocean, even if the journey is hard and uncomfortable at times.

I think this is true for us in life, too. To go deep within ourselves, to tap into our deepest desires and dreams and fears, can be daunting. But any true adventure in life requires us to go deep. As you go deeper into your craft, or a new relationship, or a new career field—whatever your personal adventure may be—you have a duty to yourself to embrace the discomfort. Stay open to your surroundings, go at your own pace, and let go of whatever could be holding you back. It's in the depths that we're transformed. It's in the depths where we find wonder.

As we journey into the unknown, the ocean reminds us that it's good to go deep within ourselves, for this is where we learn who we really are.

Who told you
you were not free
to swim wildly
into the deep?

Perhaps it was a well-meaning, worried hand
yanking your fearless body back to the shore.
"I just don't want you to drown . . ."
"I don't think you're ready yet . . ."
"I just want you to be careful."

So you backed away.
You were careful that day.
And the next day.
And for the rest of the decade.
And the next decade . . .

Years
of carefulness
all tangled up,
holding you back.

You know how to swim,
there is such thing as healthy fear,
but don't let it keep you from the waves.

Let fear wash away.
You need to go deeper here.

When I feel afraid
to wade in the deep,

when I don't allow myself to float freely
in the ocean of possibility,

when I start to worry
how to make the most of my time,

and when I fear my dreams
don't mean anything,

I look back at how far I have come
and I am reminded that I,
myself,
am the dream.

The dream of my ancestors
who were not meant to survive,
who were not meant to run
or swim in the deep
without fear
of being hunted like animals.
We were not meant to be free . . .
I am reminded
that even if all I do here
is breathe,
I have done a miraculous thing.
We have already made it
through the impossible.
We have already braved the deep.
Any movement
from this moment forward
is a continuum of bravery.

How did this world come to be?

These coral reefs
with red leaves like lungs
and spiked unnamed peaks
stretching upward
like underwater mountains,
the sight makes my heart stop.
Shelves of flora
rounded and flat, spiky and tall—
all these colors
I've never seen above the shore.
I dive deeper in pursuit of more,
and just when I think
I have reached the end of the sea,
the floor drops off,
and I descend to new depths,
only to find that this beauty
keeps going
changing
shifting
growing.

I cannot go any farther,
or I won't be able to breathe.
What's beyond will stay a mystery.

My question remains:
How did all these stories come to be?

We may never know,
but we don't have to
fully understand something
to find it beautiful.

AWAKEN YOURSELF TO
LIFE'S LITTLE MOMENTS.
BE PRESENT
TO THE INVITATIONS
TO DANCE IN
THE DEEP.

YOU ARE INVITED
TO ENGAGE
WITH SOMETHING
BIGGER THAN YOU.

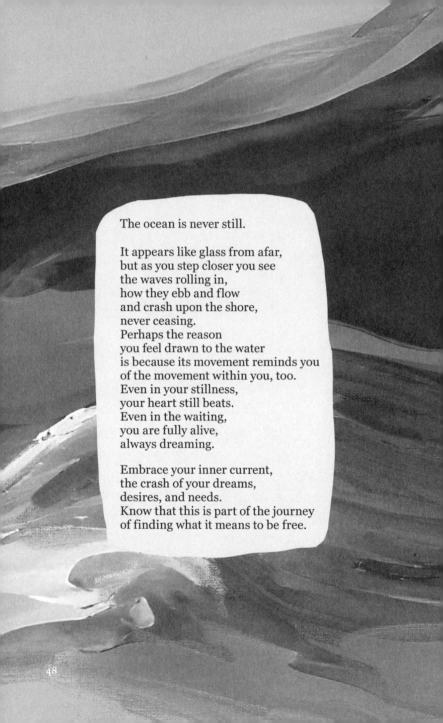

The ocean is never still.

It appears like glass from afar,
but as you step closer you see
the waves rolling in,
how they ebb and flow
and crash upon the shore,
never ceasing.
Perhaps the reason
you feel drawn to the water
is because its movement reminds you
of the movement within you, too.
Even in your stillness,
your heart still beats.
Even in the waiting,
you are fully alive,
always dreaming.

Embrace your inner current,
the crash of your dreams,
desires, and needs.
Know that this is part of the journey
of finding what it means to be free.

MAY THE DEEP BLUE
REMIND YOU
OF ALL THAT
IS LEFT TO
EXPLORE.

STAY IN BOLD PURSUIT
OF SOMETHING
DEEPER.
SOMETHING MORE.

I watch the white-capped waves break
against the shore.
The roaring sound of the sea
floods into me,
and the stormwater
pulls me into its depths.
Heavy clouds sweep my shoulders,
the wind rages against me,
and the salt burns my tongue.

The ocean reminds me
of how small I really am.
And yet, I survive.
There must be a reason I'm still here.

BE FULLY PRESENT
TO YOUR EVERYDAY
CONVERSATIONS.
WHAT COMES
TO THE SURFACE
MIGHT SURPRISE YOU.
LISTEN CLOSELY.
YOU'RE NEVER
THE ONLY ONE
SEARCHING
FOR MORE.

PAY
ATTENTION
TO WHAT
YOUR SOUL
DEEPLY
CRAVES

As you venture out into new depths,
let silence be your serenade.

You have become accustomed to clatter
and chatter
of busy people
doing busy things.

But I promise you
if you stay with the silence,
you will recognize
that your soul was made for the deep.

Not everyone else will join you
when you decide to go beyond the shallow waters.
Not everyone will understand the desire for depth
that is stirring within your heart.
When you choose to be the one
who sits with questions
and rejects simple answers,
you may hear the disappointment in the voices
of those you once looked up to.

There might be some who say you're lazy,
not doing enough.
The ones who scoff at your stillness
and still rush toward busyness above the shore,
they will not be able to meet you
on the ocean's floor.

But when you sink deeper into thought,
you will discover it is possible
to still walk with people above the surface without always
expecting them to meet you
exactly where you are.
Here in the water, you are becoming
who you are meant to be.
You are free to exchange the rush of things
for endless, boundless, peace.

When you're feeling dizzy
and you've gone too far too fast—
where hurt turns to pain,
where fear turns to anxiety,
you can only hold your breath
under water
for so long.

You need a lifeline,
something to breathe life into you
when you cannot rely
on atmospheric air alone—
     time
     therapy
     tears
     late-night talks
     with friends,
exhale, and take these in as your
oxygen.

EIGHT SIGNS YOU'RE LEARNING TO GO DEEPER

1
You're discovering beautiful things
about the world around you and about your place in it.

2
You're taking time to think before you speak.
You're allowing conversations to breathe.

3
You're learning to redefine success in a way
that makes sense for you.

4
You're finding joy in the process and allowing
more time for your ideas to flow.

5
You're enjoying quiet moments.

6
You're recognizing stillness as an integral
and good part of your story.

7
You're becoming less afraid and becoming more curious as
you face new unknowns.

8
You're making time to dream and turning
dreams into reality.

EXPLORING YOUR GIFTS

LESSONS FROM HONEYBEES

WHAT WE LEARN
FROM HONEYBEES

Every bee in a hive has a different job to do. In fact, each worker honeybee takes on four different jobs throughout its short lifetime, adopting different responsibilities within the colony. From cleaning to nursing to foraging, different skills are required for each stage of life. The harmony of the hive is dependent on the bees embracing their calling and contributing to the whole.

In life, we are invited to embrace our unique skills and giftings, too. I like to believe we're never done learning. We're never done growing. We always have more talents to try on and explore. In every adventure, we have an opportunity to become curious with ourselves and develop new skills. Maybe you'll succeed, or maybe you'll fail, but you never know what you may find out about yourself. Maybe you're a latent artist, brilliant thinker, wonderful sports player, or simply have a gift for listening. As you move forward on this new adventure, become intentional about how you're growing in your gifts. Those gifts impact the world around you.

THE SMALLEST ACTIONS
YOU TAKE HERE
MATTER MORE
THAN MOST KNOW.
IT IS THE LITTLE
ATTENTION TO DETAIL
AND COMMITMENT
TO PROGRESS
THAT HELPS
ALL OF US GROW.

WHAT IF YOU DARED
TO MAKE GOLD?

MAKE SOMETHING
BEAUTIFUL.

BE DARING IN YOUR DREAMS,
AND REMEMBER,
YOU NEVER NEED
TO ACHIEVE THEM ALONE.

A NEW WAY OF THINKING
A NEW WAY OF LIVING.
A NEW WAY OF LIVING
A MEANINGFUL LIFE.

LET THE PROCESS
BE JOYFUL
AND HARD
AND AWKWARD.

LET IT BE YOU.

She flies through a garden
unfamiliar to her.
The flowers are different here, taller here,
redder here.
The flower stems stretch into the sky,
reaching higher
than she dreamed could be possible.

It's glorious.
It's beautiful.
And at the same time she wonders,
where will she find her purpose here?
She looks for a familiar face,
a gesture,
somewhere safe to land.
It is so exhausting to be alone
and out of control.

She keeps going until
she finds her kind,
a new hive
where she can rest.

The bees begin to dance.
She knows this dance.
A code
of all the secrets
she needs to know
to feel at home.

Is there anything more generous
than dancing with one another?

Look for the ones who see you
for who you are
and welcome you in
to join in the rhythms of their lives
and share in the secrets of their hives.
And someday, you may be positioned
to share your secrets too.

TOGETHER,
WE HAVE
ENOUGH

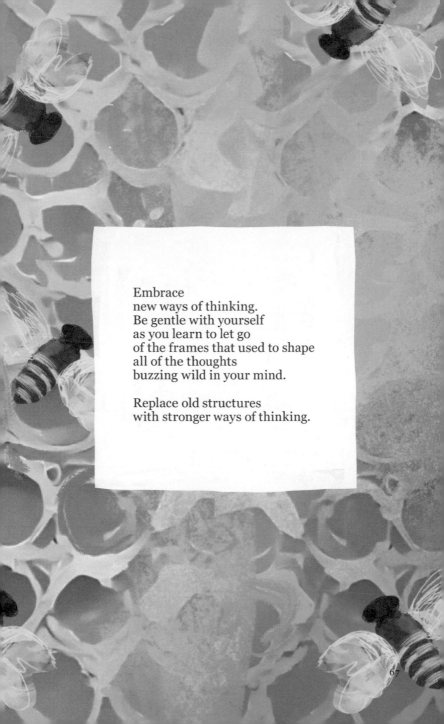

Embrace
new ways of thinking.
Be gentle with yourself
as you learn to let go
of the frames that used to shape
all of the thoughts
buzzing wild in your mind.

Replace old structures
with stronger ways of thinking.

Now is the time
to extend grace to yourself.
Now is the time to see:
Some will learn by listening,
others will learn through doing,
and some will need to revisit
the same work over and over again.

What matters is that you seek to know
the ways in which you learn
and not to feel shame
for the lessons that took
a little more time.

May you never compare
the way you learn to anyone else.
May you never judge yourself
for slower speeds.
Progress at your own pace.

Right here, right now,
pay closer attention
to what makes you *you*—
including the way
you take in something new.

The forager bee heads out in hope,
vibrating its wings
to lift itself up—
over the pink sea below.

The hosta takes a bow,
extending her open palms with grace,
inviting the lonesome bee to come and see
the golden coins she has to offer.
These nectar coins are her currency
to survive,
they are the sustenance
of an entire hive,
and this hosta shares so generously.

A light breeze lifts them all—

These pinks and greens
and yellows in motion—
it's a canvas of generosity.
Who could have imagined
this daily work
could be so beautiful?

Here's to creating
something beautiful.
Embracing
new stories,
new people,
new interests,
and colors.

This is the time to explore.
Every day you choose
to create,
you are becoming part
of something bigger than you.
You are becoming wise.
You are becoming resourceful,
letting the wind lift you as you tire,
daily practicing generosity
and resilience for the journey ahead.

SAY GOODBYE TO STRIVING FOR "EXPERT." SAY HELLO TO CURIOSITY AND INVITING OTHERS IN.

LET GO OF PERFECTION AND BRING FORTH GOODNESS

Bees are vital to our ecosystems,
and yet,
they are blissfully unaware
of the contribution they make.
They just keep doing the good work anyway.

You have no idea how far your good work will fly.
You have to learn to do the work
simply
because you love to do good.

For goodness, not glamour.
For adoration, not applause.

You are allowed to do good just because.

The hive is a collective of individuals who need one another for their survival. Like these bees, you were never meant to make your life all on your own. Whenever you start to feel that your contributions are insignificant, remember that it's only by working together that we will have all we need to become who we are called to be. We thrive as one. In order to embrace the fullness of who we might be, we must always consider who we might be *together*. Carefully and mindfully contributing each day for the good of our neighbor. This is how we find our way. Always together. It takes a village.

As I look at the honey
slowly dripping from the jar,
I feel time slow.

Oh, how wonderful it would be
if our lives were filled with such ease!

But every drip of honey
takes hours of labor to produce.
I am reminded of the peaceful work of bees
flying to and fro in rhythm with one another,
tirelessly gathering the pollen,
heaving it back home,
and storing it with care
in narrow passageways.

How often we forget the hard work
behind the sweetness.

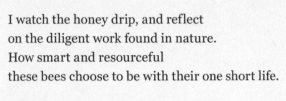

I watch the honey drip, and reflect
on the diligent work found in nature.
How smart and resourceful
these bees choose to be with their one short life.

I am choosing to seek delight
and embrace the honey moments of life
in both work and rest—
anywhere I can find it.

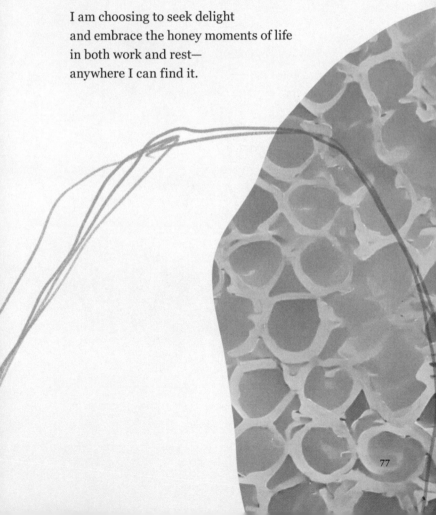

6 SIGNS YOU'RE STAYING CURIOUS AND NURTURING YOUR CREATIVE SOUL

1
You're becoming less worried about
what others think when you share your ideas.

2
You're seeking new ways of problem-solving,
stemming from your hope for the future.

3
You're discovering new passions
that you will talk about for hours.

4
You're noticing your inner critic
is not as loud as it used to be.

5
You're falling in love with
the process of making things.

6
Your curiosity is piqued as to
where the journey might lead.

EMBRACING YOUR EMOTIONS

LESSONS FROM GUITARS

WHAT WE LEARN FROM GUITARS

A guitar is just some hollowed-out wood, a few strings, and some pegs. Individually, no single component seems particularly special. But with some craftsmanship and skill, all of these parts come into alignment to create what I believe to be one of the most beautiful objects mankind has ever made. When I hold a guitar, I feel like I come alive. With a simple stroke of the hand, I can strike a chord, and music fills the room. People inevitably turn their heads. They can't help it. Music is powerful.

Music isn't something we can see, or touch, or smell. But we are so affected by it. *How can we be so swayed by something we cannot observe?*

I often think the same thing about our emotions. We are not always able to see or fully understand where our emotions are coming from, but they play such a commanding role in our lives. Sometimes they're out of tune, and we find it jarring. We find ourselves begging our minds to please turn down the music. It's too much, too loud. Other times, we're longing hear a song again within us, but that song doesn't come. Sometimes, however, when we find that perfect song inside and express true emotions, it feels like we're at a concert made just for us. We find ourselves more vulnerable and open to others. No matter how well or poorly we play those chords, it's evident when we're in tune with ourselves. We have learned how to strike those chords all on our own.

At every stage of the journey ahead, emotions will rise and fall, and we owe it to ourselves to let them pass through us, as we learn to enjoy this ever-changing song.

Like music,
your emotions
are meant to be expressed
and explored.
Follow what is unpredictable.

You might feel tempted to hold back
when you are not sure
if the chords you will play
will come out the right way,
but it matters
so try to play anyway.

You might be afraid of
how others will respond
when you play out of tune
and when your melancholy
strikes the chord
much harder than you meant for it to,
but the truth is,
even if others don't like the music
of who you are,
you must let it echo anyway,
for it is real, it is yours.

There will be times
when regret will rise up within you
like a dissonant song
that pains your ears to hear,

like a harsh melody
played with strings out of tune—
but this remains true:
within the very same day,
other songs are playing, too.

Just as that sound moves through the room,
let these emotions move through you, too.

Just simply be
with the music of this moment.

Retune.
And let go.

WRITE NEW SONGS. CHANGE YOUR LIFE.

Let today be the day you allow your joy
to be loud and unapologetic.

There are birds in the backyard,
singing of springtime sunshowers.

The tree's branches,
nature's drum kit,
play their new leaves.

Rain crashes
like cymbals into puddles below.

Music
all around us,
each and every day . . .
And I know there is music in you, too.

Here's to embracing life's song
one small moment of joy at a time.
Let us unapologetically
enjoy the sounds
of this ongoing symphony.

The sounds of joy and sorrow
reverberate in the air around us,
two songs always playing.

We will be swooned
by the delight
of new beginnings,
but find ourselves weeping
when we realize that means
we have to let go
in order to grow.

But the more we live,
the more we will find
that it's about finding
how we make those songs
pair well
together.

We learn to sing
with gracious strength,
singing of our pain
and all the good we've gained
by embracing the full tone
and range of notes
that life has brought us.

Sometimes you don't know
where the song comes from,

somewhere deep within your soul.

But it comes, and you have to play.
It overtakes you,
and now,
you're along for the ride.

The Deep South origins of jazz
        double bass
        backbeats
        rhythms that swing
        your heart
        to believe
        you're free

//key change//

Now folk music
        telling stories,
        the chords
        open up

                    to catch
              a falling
        memory,
              and now that memory
              is safe
              and warm
              in the arms of a song
              of homecoming

//key change//

To the blues
        because
        coming home
        ain't always easy
        rhythm is found
        in the repetition
        of your lament,
        through the blues
        you bring it forward,
        you let the troubles breathe

        breathe

WITH EVERY CHORD PROGRESSION, THERE IS A PROGRESSION OF YOU

When is the heart ready for love?
When is the heart ready to tune to another?

Love is patient,
love is kind,
sound truth
that is also a mystery.
Sacred,
sought after,
a bellowing hum
through history,
alive in the mountains,
the valleys,
and all of the places in between.
Over and over love sings
welcoming melodies
for every heart that beats.

When is the heart ready for love?
When is the heart ready to tune to another?

Perhaps, it is when the heart decides
love will always be greater than oneself,
and to love at all is to encounter Divine Presence
in relationship with someone else.

I CANNOT HOLD THE SONG OR TOUCH IT WITH MY HANDS. BUT I BELIEVE WE ALL HAVE A SONG PLAYING ON IN THE LINING OF OUR HEARTS.

PAY ATTENTION

TO THE SUBTLE WAYS

THAT JOY

PULLS AT THE

HEARTSTRINGS.

FROM WITHIN THE HOLLOW BODY
OF AN ACOUSTIC GUITAR,
MUSIC RISES UP TO THE SURFACE
AND FILLS THE ROOM.
ISN'T IT A MIRACLE HOW
SOMETHING SO STRIKING
CAN RISE UP OUT OF NOTHING?

JOY FULLY EMBODIED HEALS

Let us travel away from the city and go
where green fields grow untouched and free.
Where the wind is music
and the horizon line
is a guitar's string.

Let us hum the tune of gratitude
as we cross paths
with those we meet.

And let us walk together,
our feet becoming our instruments,
a song of togetherness.
Compassion so loud
it cannot possibly be ignored.

It is good when we sing
in harmony,
our differences
a felt reality,
as real as the
ground beneath our feet.

Together, a song much richer,
sweeter,
and stronger
than any melody
I could write on my own.

May there be peace between people,
and peace beyond understanding.
May there be places in nature
where souls feel free
to roam and simply be.

Take me there.

GET IN THE FLOW.
LOSE TRACK
OF TIME.
ALLOW
YOURSELF
TO BE
ONE WITH
YOUR
EMOTIONS.

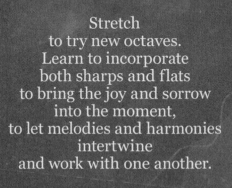

Stretch
to try new octaves.
Learn to incorporate
both sharps and flats
to bring the joy and sorrow
into the moment,
to let melodies and harmonies
intertwine
and work with one another.

The way we write new music
is by exploring new ways
to work with each note.

6 SIGNS YOU'RE LEARNING TO FULLY EMBRACE YOUR EMOTIONS WITHOUT SHAME

1
You're learning to welcome good feelings and bad.

2
You know with confidence that your feelings do not make you weak.

3
You're allowing yourself to feel your emotions as they arise and allowing them to pass through you.

4
You're beginning to see that experiencing negative emotions can still lead to a healthy, open-hearted version of yourself.

5
You're realizing that your unique emotional experience is to be honored.

6
You're learning to trust your emotions as truth-tellers in your life, and you value your feelings to inform your next step on the journey.

NAVIGATING YOUR TRIALS

LESSONS FROM LIONS

WHAT WE LEARN FROM LIONS

In our history, in our literature, and in our fairy tales, lions have become synonymous with strength. We think of them as majestic, formidable, unrivaled rulers of their land. However, lions run into predators and face challenges, too. They can have a swarm of hyenas surrounding them in minutes. Even though they're one of the boldest animals, they still must be wise and seek out safety. They must learn to be aware, astute, always on guard. They have to be judicious with how they navigate each trial, whether to show force or retreat in safety.

There are times in our lives when we will need to be lionhearted—to have courage to navigate truly grueling trials. Like the lion, we have to find the best way to navigate hardship and even real danger. There will be moments when we cannot be passive. When we find ourselves deep in the trenches, we must learn to fight and look out for one another. Awareness and discernment will lead us through the decision of whether to roar or to run, but we must remember, neither option is necessarily weak. We must simply seek what is wise.

The day has finally come for you.
You can feel it in your bones:
You are stronger
than you have ever been.
You hear
your mother's
roar in your ear,
reminding you
that you are more than capable
of carrying on in this journey.
You've come so far
and now is
the time for you to be
the bold, resilient soul
you were made to be.
You can do anything.

A rustle in the grass.
The eyes of a predator
glow like fireflies through the brush.
You scan your surroundings for more
because you know, out here, predators do not travel alone.
They'll encircle you in an instant,
suffocating you with their laughs.

They know you are strong,
but they also know you are alone,
and your strength is weakened now.

But you were not naive.
You knew your journey would be perilous,
and you have been preparing for this.

Instinct takes over
and it's time to run,
to leap,
high
fast
faster now.
You don't stop.
You narrowly escape.

You have brushed up against death,
much closer than you ever wanted to.
That felt much worse than you expected.

You don't take it lightly that you got away.
There will be more predators,
but rest easy now, quiet your thoughts.
You are safe another day.

You don't have to figure it out all alone.
You must be kind to yourself.
And it is okay to take your time
as you learn to keep going.

Resilience is a learned practice.
To stay on the road
and be confronted with discomfort.
It is natural to retreat
and let them beat
you back to where you came from.

But the art of coming back
to the road
is something you can practice.

Bravery is earned.

Storm clouds will roll in.
Your patience will wear thin.
And you will start to wonder
if this treacherous journey
is even worth it.

Through it all,
honor your humanity:
    imperfect,
    vulnerable,
    and flawed.
And honor your ability
to get back up again.

DON'T BE

ASHAMED

OF THE

FEAR

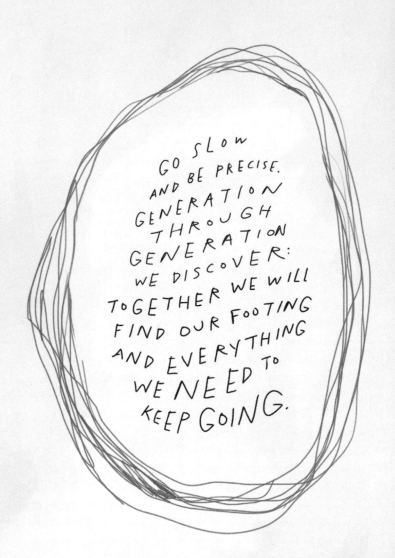

GO SLOW
AND BE PRECISE.
GENERATION
THROUGH
GENERATION
WE DISCOVER:
TOGETHER WE WILL
FIND OUR FOOTING
AND EVERYTHING
WE NEED TO
KEEP GOING.

IT'S

NOT

YOUR

FAULT

The lioness watches her cubs run and play
knowing that someday,
they will encounter trials of their own.
Even though she has worked to protect her family,
she knows that someday they will stare down
threats, as have all of their ancestors.
And it is hard not to imagine how things might worsen.
She has known the pain of what it means to watch a
community shrink.
She racks her mind for all the ways she must prepare them,
anticipating threats that she has yet to know.
So she trains them.
She trains them to be fierce and to be alert,
to be strong and look out for one another,
to never forget the enduring strength of a village,
to never underestimate the power of their roar.

To wander
through the unknown
is unsettling,
and all you want
are the answers.
Answers keep us safe.
But what if you let go
of needing all the answers
and embrace the dangerous task
of asking questions?

EVERY TRIAL
IS AN
OPPORTUNITY
TO SUMMON
THE POWER
OF YOUR
PRIDE

"How did I get here?"
A question you often ask yourself
at the rugged edges of starless nights.

Dear friend,

You are a human
doing hard human things.
And that's how you got here.

And to get where you are going next,
    perhaps, you'll never be ready.
        And yet, you still have to go.

This is not the end of your journey,
it is not going to be this hard forever.

Ask yourself:
What can I let go of?
What boundaries can I put in place?
Am I expecting perfection?

Remember why you started on this journey.
    Breathe through the rest.

HERE'S TO
LEARNING HOW
TO BREATHE IN
AND OUT:
"I WILL
GET THROUGH THIS"

Sometimes anticipating loss
can feel just as heavy
as the loss itself.

And in our world,
to grieve properly often requires
planning
plane tickets for the funeral,
donating worn clothes,
wills,
and lawyers,
and now,
in this absence,
you can't just call
and say
"Hello . . ."
or ask where all of the shoes should go.

Grief
has suddenly changed
your life
and all you hoped you would be.

And then,
worry, grief's loyal companion,
preys upon your heart.

Even though this darkness
has left you feeling alone,
if you look and listen closer,
you will discover:
There are others here
who feel what you feel.

We learn to make the most of our time
and embrace one another
through both loss and love.

MAY YOU NEVER
TELL YOURSELF
YOUR SUFFERING
IS NOT THAT SERIOUS.
MAY YOU NEVER THINK
YOU DON'T NEED CARE
BECAUSE SOMEONE ELSE
NEEDS IT MORE THAN YOU.

WHATEVER YOUR
HEART NEEDS
TO RETURN TO
PATTERNS
OF PEACE
IS ALWAYS
WORTH PURSUING.

TAKE HEART,
BREATHE DEEP.
TO BE ALIVE
IS A
MIRACULOUS
FEAT.

8 THINGS YOU LEARN
WHEN NAVIGATING TRIALS

1

You learn to pay attention.

2

You learn to identify the signals for safe and unsafe people
and places.

3

You find that some paths seem littered with predators,
and that's okay. You are allowed to turn around in pursuit
of another way.

4

You learn that when daylight has left the sky,
new fears might come alive,
and it's best for you to take shelter and rest.
Pace yourself for the fight.

5

You find that you are not alone out here. You seek out trusted friends.

6

You learn not to blame yourself for the things that happen to you.

7

You're courageous enough to admit you need help from those you love.

8

You refuse to let other people's words, opinions, and attacks on you keep you from the journey you're called to.

BEGINNING AGAIN

LESSONS FROM CLIMBING ROSES

WHAT WE LEARN FROM CLIMBING ROSES

Unlike most roses, the climbing rose blooms multiple times within a season, and nearly all varieties are perennial, flowering again year after year. While the roses only bloom for approximately half the year, the plant must be cared for with gentleness all year long. The climbing rose responds uniquely well to training, and it will grow upward along surfaces, walls, and trellises, as long as it's guided to.

Much like the climbing rose, whether we're in a season of flourishing or a season of drought, we owe it to ourselves to approach our stories with tenderness and care all the year long. We have the responsibility to prune our lives and train our hearts to climb, as they were meant to.

While we can't always control the seasons, we do have the ability to adapt and make changes in each season so that we can continue to carry on. Right here, you can choose to plan out the path of your growth, and as you set out into your future, you must give yourself permission to start again. To climb higher and higher than you ever have before. The longer we live, the more stories we are likely to collect about heartbreak and disappointment, but the climbing rose gives us hope that it is possible for goodness to return. Rising up even in the hardest, longest seasons, we can always begin again.

I am learning that the beauty
of the climbing rose
is that it blooms
again and again and again.
I take delight to gaze upon
the fullness
of its beauty at every stage,
from the first springtime bud
to its branches
stretching outward.
Every petal unfolds
only to eventually wither away
until another day.

"It will come back someday."
This is what I say
to the young boy
standing at my side.
As he tilts his head to the side,
so does the rose.
"Just wait, it's coming back,
it's going to bloom again."
The words are for him,
and I am telling
this to myself, too.
The roses always
bloom back
how they were meant to.

YOU STEP ASIDE
READY TO BRING
YOUR GARDEN BACK TO LIFE.
THE FIRST ACT
TO MAKING THIS PLACE BEAUTIFUL
IS RIPPING IT APART.
RIPPING UP THE WEEDS
AND PRUNING BACK
ALL THAT NO LONGER
SERVES US.
AND WITH EACH ROOT
WE UNCOVER
WE'RE BRINGING FORTH
A VIBRANT INNER HOPE
FOR TOMORROW.

The climbing rose spent all winter
in silent meditation,
nurturing the belief
that the sky is the limit.

And today, after months of hard work,
digging her roots deep,
today,
she blooms.

Welcome back to the garden,
you exquisite rose.
Welcome back to the process
of making and building and breathing.
It looks different this year than it did last year,
  more color
  higher heights
  deeper roots.
The hard work you've been doing
is shining through.

WHENEVER
YOU START
TO FEEL
YOU HAVE
MISSED OUT
ON LOVE,
REMEMBER THIS—

FOR ALL OF THE
THINGS IN LIFE
THAT ONLY HAVE ONE BLOOM,
LOVE WILL CONTINUE
TO BLOOM AGAIN
WITHIN YOU.

WHO YOU
HAVE BECOME
TODAY IS UNIQUE
TO THE WORLD YOU
HAVE KNOWN. YOUR
PERSEVERANCE HAS
MADE YOU COLORFUL
AND VIBRANT WITH
GLORIOUS SUNRAYS
OF A NEW DAY AND
HOPE FOR
TOMORROW.

LIKE EVERY PETAL
SLOWLY UNFOLDING
IN SPRINGTIME BLOOM,
MAY THAT LITTLE
BUD OF COURAGE
UNFOLD INSIDE YOU, TOO

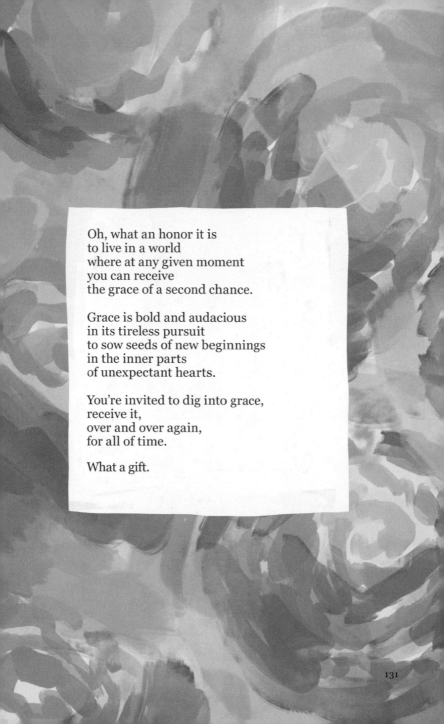

Oh, what an honor it is
to live in a world
where at any given moment
you can receive
the grace of a second chance.

Grace is bold and audacious
in its tireless pursuit
to sow seeds of new beginnings
in the inner parts
of unexpectant hearts.

You're invited to dig into grace,
receive it,
over and over again,
for all of time.

What a gift.

MAY THE FLOWERS
GROW WILD AND FREE,
AND MAY GRACE
ADORN
ABSOLUTELY
EVERYTHING.

AS A GARDENER,
YOU KNOW
NOT ALL OF YOUR ROSES
WILL MAKE IT TO BLOOM.
AND YOU ALSO KNOW
THE ONES
CUT OUT
WILL MAKE ROOM
FOR NEW ROSES
TO GROW.

You might not know
how to feel
about the thorns
that have grown
on the stems of your story,
you might not know
how to speak firmly
about the boundaries
you have learned to set . . .
but you are learning
it does not make you weak
to set limits
in your life.
In fact,
it makes you wise.

BEGINNING AGAIN
STARTS WITH THE
SIMPLE ACT
OF TURNING
YOUR FACE
TO THE HORIZON
AND CHOOSING
SUNLIGHT.

Over and over you rise above
the obstacles you thought
would hold you back.
And each time,
you were learning to start again.
Each time,
you were learning to breathe deep
and trust:
This is not the end.

To espalier your roses—
the practice
of controlling woody plant growth
to grow within a frame
to give them something to rest against—

After everything you've been through,
that's exactly what you need.
A little time to welcome rest
in the light of possibility
of growing upward,
taking up space,
flourishing.

BE PATIENT WITH YOUR ROSES
FOR THEY CAN TAKE
YEARS TO GROW.

A NEW BEGINNING CAN CHANGE EVERYTHING, WHICH IS WHY YOU MUST LET THEM BLOOM AND COME IN SLOWLY.

GIVE THEM TIME AND GIVE THEM HOPE.

7 SIGNS YOU'RE READY TO START AGAIN AFTER DISAPPOINTMENT

1
You're recognizing that starting over doesn't mean being perfect.

2
You're accepting that failure is not weak.

3
You're starting to identify, with clarity,
how you have learned from where you have been,
and you're even open to sharing it with others.

4
You are not pretending that the past never happened.
You are finding gratitude in your experiences and looking to
the future.

5
You're making changes without feeling like you need to
explain yourself.

6
You're pursuing new passions and projects, just because.

7
You're finding freedom
in being faithful where you are,
and you've learned to hold your plans lightly.

EMBRACING CHANGE

LESSONS FROM
SPACE

WHAT WE LEARN FROM SPACE

When I look at the stars, I often feel quiet, at peace. I rest on the backyard fence, my feet planted on the ground, and everything seems still. It's easy to think of the sky as one big black canvas with a few fixed stars, but the reality is, the universe is in a dance of forceful, ordered chaos, swirling all around me—always expanding, moving at speeds of 552,000 miles per hour. The universe you and I live in is in constant flux, on the grandest of scales. But from where I stand, it's nearly imperceptible. Every star I can see is actually just an image of the past—already dead for at least 10,000 years. I could live 140 times over before I see that light fade. Change is constant, but it's not always easy to comprehend.

We may feel small in comparison to the miraculous movement that is unceasing in space, but this remains true: Just as space is in a continual stage of change, the same is true of you. Change is inevitable—an every-moment process—even when we cannot see it within ourselves. We may not always feel like we are progressing, but when we look back on our stories, we will notice that *change* is actually one of the few constants in our lives.

For some of us, that can feel frightening. Like we're out of control. And I'm here to tell you, in some ways, yes. You are not in control. You're part of a big, wild, wondrous, and horrifying world. The moment we choose to accept that our lives are like the galaxies—in nonstop flux—the more we can begin to embrace the ebb and flow of our lives. Only then will we see that we are capable of surviving and even thriving in the face of the unknown.

WHAT IS
CHANGE?
A FORCE OF
MOVEMENT
THROUGH TIME
AND SPACE.
WE CAN ONLY
TRULY EMBRACE
THE BEAUTY OF
CHANGE
WHEN WE LET
START TO
GO OF OUR
FEARS.

145

I tried to paint the universe,
and surrendered,
with paint dripping from my hands.

Every studied stroke
and color crafted with precision—
they all failed me.
I am only left
with hues of supernova on my fingertips,
asteroids on my feet.
The painting is incomplete.

I cannot comprehend the skies.

But I will keep the paint
on me
and let this ever-expanding mystery
shape my hands and my feet.
I delight that I cannot comprehend.

I will embrace the beauty of infinity
and choose awe of the changing mystery.

Sunrise, sunset,
the earth performs
her daily pirouettes.

Like a ballerina
in constant motion,
every day,
every season,
revolving around the sun.
Orchestrated through space
alongside billions of stars,
who are also in motion,
4,000 new stars born each day.

And yet,
you wake up
and close your eyes,
day after day,
you feel stuck.
Your heart aches
for something more,
something new,
some kind of shift
that reminds you
you are human.

Oh, how easy it is
to forget you are
always moving forward,
part of the mystery.

No matter how many days feel the same,
you are part of a revolution of constant change.

I want to stretch up my arms
to the dark sky and
feel the heat of a billion stars
burning bright into life.
I want to feel like fire.
I want to be up close to changing things.
I want to feel the lava-hued Mars dust
rush to graze my skin
and watch the lightning of Venus
erupt over the iced surface.
I want to stretch my heart
up to the sky and cry,
Oh, God, how could it be,
in this expansive universe,
you could possibly see me?

It's a mystery to me.

For I know this space I live in
is filled with constant change,
but the crowded white boxes
on my calendar
are beginning to look and feel the same.
I cannot help but wonder
what lies above and beyond,
I cannot help but wonder
what it would be like
to go on
millions of miles
away from here,

to where I have never been before,
to shoot up into the sky
into the match-lit cloud
secured for me,
in my own personal rocket ship
of Always-Wanting-More,
praying it doesn't catch fire
due to sheer pressure
of my own anxious hunger.

But my rocket ship stays unfinished
here on the ground,
and slowly, the night fades,
and in the matter of a few hours,
the fire of the sun
rises to fill my windowpane.
I am reminded of the constant change
ignited in the everyday.
I will learn to see its beauty.
I will learn to take it in.
Stretch my arms up and turn to the light,
and watch the sun
set fire to hairs on my skin.

May bold, radiant hope
be ignited from within.

I cannot tell you why,
but when I look up
to the night sky
and watch the meteor shower
rushing through
the night above my head,
it feels deeply personal,
as if the show
is for me.
Streams of cosmic debris
dancing so I could see.
High-speed light
coming and going
like racing cars
on a celestial highway.
My eyes,
my heart,
my camera
cannot keep up.
All I can do is look up
and feel that maybe
I am free
to believe
in this moment,
this celestial race is
just for me.

Dear friend,
please know:
You may feel you are aimlessly
drifting,
consumed by the cosmos
forgotten
floating through space
lost, drifting—
but when I see you, I know
you are like a fleck of star dust
on the brink of
bursting into brightness,
and there is a place for you
planned for you,
right here, in this very space.
Your light has always shone
and will only continue to grow.

Take this time to ask,
to seek, to know
who you are
and who you could be
as you constantly move
through the atmosphere.

Crack your knuckles.
Roll your neck.
Square your shoulders.
Take your first step
onto the launchpad.
Your suit is heavy and stiff on your body,
but your spirit is light
with the hope of what could be.

Is it scary?
Perhaps,
but you would not have made it here
to this point had you not learned
to keep your hope, despite your fears.

You're the first one in your family
to take this trip.
You'll be the first to come back,
holding the story of
the universe in your hands.

And some young dreamer
watching you today
will stand tomorrow
where you are standing today,
launching farther and
farther into space.
You lit a match of what you hope
will be a mighty flame
of constant change.

All of your fears of
inadequacy wash away,
and you focus on the task,
standing firm in this place
to make a way for more.

For you are the change.
Remember all it took to get here.
You,
yes you,
are the change.

When you gaze back toward Earth
and gain perspective on its complexity
and majesty
hung in the midst of nothingness
and all of the life and people and stories
it holds—
you realize how precious it is,
a place
worth cherishing,
worth cultivating.

Your compassion grows.
Your love expands.
You come back to the ground
and you fight for Earth's best end.

You've been divinely plucked
out of obscurity
for this time, this space,
and by Grace brought forth
so you might live these years
and learn from them.

Let your mind and heart
be forever shaped
by all the mystery
that is continually,
faithfully,
being revealed to you.

I've seen galaxies incomprehensible.
Divinity's love letter
of sweeping hues
purple and blue,
stars hung like beads
bejeweling the sky.
The Light is now forever with me,
and everything I see is changed by it.

Returning home,
I try to speak of it,
but my words cannot contain
the majesty.

Confused eyes stare back in judgment,
disinterest.
"Sounds nice," they say.
I drop my eyes, ashamed.
But I see how the star dust still glazes my hands.
I clasp them together.
It's all I have left.

Until the mirror reminds me
of the Light in my eye—
Divinity's painting
is now hung there,
glistening gold specks,
forever bright.
Gravity may hold me down,
and others may leer,
but no matter what they say or do,
I know I have been made new.

I can keep my feet
on the ground
while knowing
I am forever changed.

EVERYTHING AROUND YOU SPINS. BUT YOU ARE FINDING CLARITY WITHIN. MAY THE NEVER-ENDING CHANGES IN YOUR LIFE BE A CATALYST TO BECOME A MORE COURAGEOUS YOU.

I stand light-years away
from what they call
the Pillars of Creation.

I see them,
and I'll be honest,
I am afraid.

My mind couldn't fathom
the possibility
of elephant trunk constellations,
these roaring,
jagged lights rising
into black night.

But here they stand, majestic.

I tremble at the thought
that I am of creation myself.

How does it hold together?
How do I hold together?

It's a lot of pressure.
It's a lot
to take in.

But while I wait for my Fearlessness
to disappear,
I invite Awe and Wonder
to stand alongside it.

I will trust I'll be transformed
in the Presence
of Greatness.

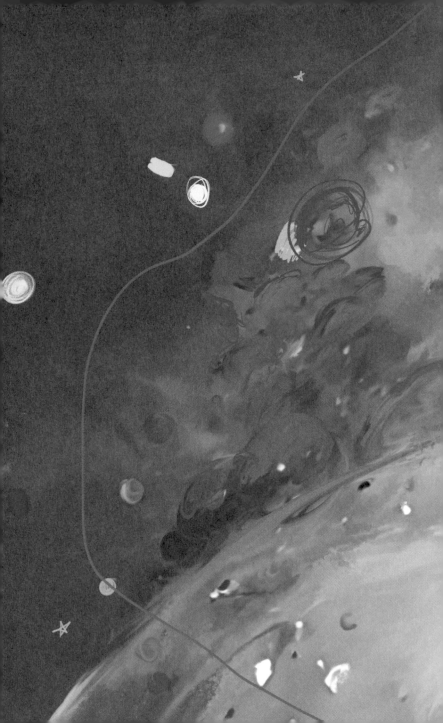

5 THINGS YOU LEARN FROM CHANGE

1
You are not who you used to be, and that is a beautiful thing.

2
Slow change is still change.

3
Change is happening all around you and within you, no matter who does or does not see it.

4
You cannot control how others respond when you start to make changes in your life, but you can manage your expectations and trust you know who you are.

5
Change is rarely easy, but challenge cultivates courage.

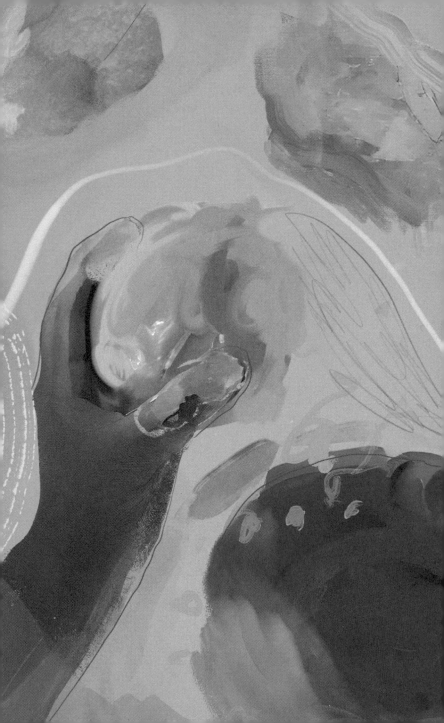

FORGIVING YOURSELF

LESSONS FROM CLAY

WHAT WE LEARN FROM CLAY

For the artist who chooses to slow down and look closely, there is no ugliness that cannot be redeemed. One of the most wonderful mediums with which to work is clay. Clay is one of the oldest materials in human history. It's one of the most malleable, too, which means it is easy to form and reform. Its plasticity makes it easy to maneuver, whether you're making a vessel or a statue, and if you are dissatisfied with your work, you can always start again. Every iteration of the clay's shape is an opportunity for the potter to learn. And yes, the potter's hands may grow coarse and tired, but every time she returns to her wheel, she has an opportunity to make something even more beautiful than before.

I like to think of my life's story as clay. Every adventure is bound to come with mistakes, some big and some small. If you ever feel like you made a mess of yourself, you may feel like your story is set in stone. Like you can't ever forgive yourself. You might see the past as fixed, with no room for a new way of seeing that chapter of your life. Mistakes, failures, and what-went-wrongs are inevitable. But what's important is that we learn from them. This is what forgiving ourselves looks like. Forgiving ourselves is recognizing that feelings and attitudes toward ourselves don't have permanent shapes, and like clay, we are allowed to change the shape of our pasts into something new, beautiful, magnificent, and maybe even purposeful.

Come and observe.
Come and see the gallery of your life.
Isn't it a bit frightening
to see your fingerprints?
The spiderweb veins that run through the clay?
The dents, the grooves, chipped edges, and stains?
So much you should have done differently.

Should.
There's that word, again.

I sit down again at the potter's wheel,
as my regrets and mistakes cast shadows on my face.

I place a new pile of clay before me.

Maybe I was just doing what I could at the time.
Perhaps I can say, "Thank you, Past,
for teaching me who I don't want to be anymore."
Maybe I can learn from where I've been—
tucked in the carvings of all that I carelessly sculpted,
there is wisdom. There is growth.
There are lessons I can carry with me today.
I get to do this. I get to look back.
I get to look back to what went wrong,
learn from it all,
and heal.

And I press my foot on the pedal
and start again.

Forgiving yourself is not erasure.
Forgiving yourself is slowing down to see
what happened for what it really was.
It's saying to yourself,
Oh, I see that I have done this thing.
I see who I was.

Yes, that's who I was.
And now I will choose who I will become.

Forgiving yourself is saying,
I'm choosing to accept consequences for that,
but I'm not going to punish myself anymore.
I'm choosing to acknowledge
that I live in a world where my actions affect others.
For better or for worse,
we all affect each other.

I look back on my life and I see streaks of jealousy,
judgment,
and resentment.
I see a shape of my soul I hardly recognize today.

But I still have power to mold this story.
I cannot erase the marks I've made.
But I can move forward to make new ones.

A coffee mug chipped at the lip.
A lopsided bowl ajar on my shelf.
A ceramic spoon set
that looks like a pile of twigs.

They haunt and humble you.
They are not what you meant to make.
But what matters is that you are kind
to the former version of yourself
who cared so much for them.

You're so tired
from having to spend your days
searching and scouring
for any bit of clay
you can find along the riverbed.
Your fingernails are lined with dirt,
your knees stained with grass
from the hours you've spent
gathering small clumps,
separating out rocks and dirt and worms.
You know what it's like to work and yearn,
to make something of what you've been given.

And you look around and see
so many artists with their purified clay,
lab-tested, perfected, purified clay.

How could you ever make what they can?

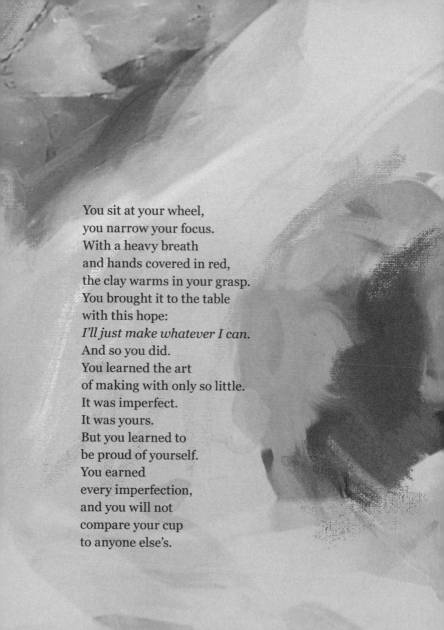

You sit at your wheel,
you narrow your focus.
With a heavy breath
and hands covered in red,
the clay warms in your grasp.
You brought it to the table
with this hope:
I'll just make whatever I can.
And so you did.
You learned the art
of making with only so little.
It was imperfect.
It was yours.
But you learned to
be proud of yourself.
You earned
every imperfection,
and you will not
compare your cup
to anyone else's.

When you can't make
the memories disappear,
work them.
Wedge them like clay,
prepare them in your hands,
turn them,
let bitterness fly away
and let what's left transform like a wave
and take on a new dynamic shape.
Clay can remember, and you must, too.
But you don't have to
let that memory define you.
Continue with this healing practice
of making old memories new.

FORGIVENESS MAKES NEW MEMORIES.

WHEN IT
STARTS TO FEEL
LIKE EVERYTHING
MIGHT FALL APART,
MAY QUIET,
RESTFUL MOMENTS
AWAY FROM THE
NOISE OF DAY
BE A BALM
FOR YOUR HEART.

SLOW DOWN.
YOU HAVE TIME.
YOU HAVE TIME.
YOU HAVE TIME
TO LEARN THE
PRACTICE
OF FORGIVING
YOURSELF.

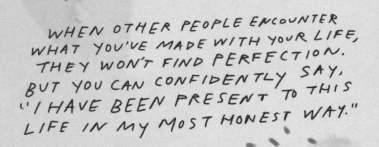

WHEN OTHER PEOPLE ENCOUNTER
WHAT YOU'VE MADE WITH YOUR LIFE,
THEY WON'T FIND PERFECTION.
BUT YOU CAN CONFIDENTLY SAY,
"I HAVE BEEN PRESENT TO THIS
LIFE IN MY MOST HONEST WAY."

When you step into the studio
and you see your unfinished,
flawed creations
side by side,
you're going to see clumps of clay
and fallen pieces
that might make you feel ashamed.

But you must remember:
You are standing in a gallery of monuments
of your memories.
Be gentle with yourself
as you gather wisdom.
Receive grace
one moment,
one day at a time.

No,
you have not lived a perfectly crafted life,
but this clay is forgiving.
These memories of your life
have not been sent through the fire.
They have not been set in stone.
These moments are still moldable.
There is still room for new shapes
to find their way in this studio.
There is still time for you to step back,
soften these edges,
find humility,
and find peace.

When you hold the clay in your hands,
you must not judge it.
You must learn to see
this moment for what it is.
A moment to create.
A moment you will learn from,
no matter what direction things go.
Go within
and ask yourself,
"What can I make now?
What beautiful things—not perfect things—
can I bring to life?
What can I make
that I will look back on
with gratitude
and peace,
knowing that I'm faithfully
stepping into who I was meant to be?"

YOUR
LIFE IS
NOT AS
SET AS
YOU
THINK.

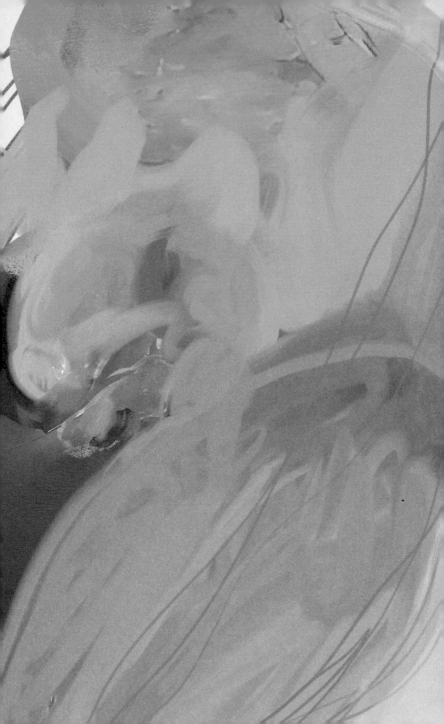

5 LESSONS YOU LEARN FROM FORGIVING YOURSELF

1

Forgiveness is one of the hardest things
you will ever do, and yet it's one
of the most rewarding, too.

2

You're not stuck in who you were.

3

Your environment will influence you,
but it doesn't define you.

4

You are allowed to let the
past take on new shapes.

5

You are free to make new shapes, too.

REINTEGRATING WITH WHERE YOU'VE COME FROM

LESSONS FROM BUTTERFLIES

WHAT WE LEARN FROM
MONARCH BUTTERFLIES

Every year, monarch butterflies migrate from as far north as Canada to as far south as Mexico. Their migration is different from other migrating species because they only live for a few weeks. It takes many generations of these butterflies to make one full trip. Due to their life span, they don't get to see the whole migration path all the way through, but they know they are part of something bigger than themselves. Each of their small, individual journeys sums to a much larger journey than any single butterfly's.

The monarch butterfly migration is a reminder that each of our stories is part of an even bigger story. Our stories pave the way for one another to take flight on each journey. Our stories are sources of inspiration for others.

At the close of any journey, we have a responsibility to reconcile our new changed selves with our ideas of who we were and where we came from. When we change emotionally, spiritually, physically, you name it—we have to realize that we have now changed the entire ecosystem we're living in. We have to reintegrate our new selves with our home, and we have to allow that home to grow and change, too.

Recognize that you've done the good, wonderful, hard work of stepping out in ways you never knew were possible. Maybe you accomplished what you wanted. Maybe not. But either way, you've been transformed by the journey, and now it's time to reintegrate, reconcile, pass the baton, and share the goodness you've gained.

In humility, faith, and hope, welcome home.

WHAT GREATER JOURNEY
ARE WE WILLING
TO BE PART OF
EVEN IF IT'S ONLY
FOR A LIMITED TIME?
EVEN IF IT'S SOMEONE ELSE
WHO LIVES TO SEE
THE FINISH LINE?

Reintegrating with
where you've come from
is the act of honoring
the person you were
and the person you've become.
You move about the world
with new colors now
after flights of fancy
high in the skies
to low moments
barely hovering above the earth.
You've changed
metamorphized
grown.

Coming home helps you begin to see
you've come so far
and who you really are.
A future you
never thought was possible.

YOUR INNER FLAME
BURNS MORE BRIGHTLY NOW,
PERMEATING THROUGH
YOUR SKIN.

YOUR CONVICTION
IS PRESENT IN ALL YOU TOUCH.
YOU LIVE LESS AFRAID.

YOU SHINE
LIKE GOLD,
POISED TO LIVE
IN THIS NEW MAGNIFICENCE
FOR THE REST OF
YOUR LIFE.

We are continually working for the good of others. The seeds we sow today will be appreciated by others tomorrow. The stories we tell today might become part of a survival guide for the people we pass the baton to. I only hope I can give her a secret or two to make it a bit easier. We choose to be present not only for ourselves but for the beautiful stories unfolding around us.

TAKE TIME TO DISCOVER
THE LINK BETWEEN
REST AND RENEWAL.
SETTLE FOR A MOMENT
WHERE THE FLOWERS GROW
OR IN THE COMFORTING SOUND OF RAIN
PATTERING AGAINST YOUR BEDROOM WINDOW.
LET A SLOWER PACE FIND YOU
AND RETURN
RESTED, RENEWED, RESTORED.

Look for the teachers in your life.

They may be your friends,
or they may be your failures.

Books you only finished halfway.
Unreconciled disagreements.
The one who got away.

I hope that if it is possible,
you can see your failures as teachers, too.
And all of the people who disappointed you.

There are so many lessons you've learned on your journey,
so many unexpected paths and roads you had to take,
trials that made you awake
to who you were meant to be.
You're wiser now.
Look around and ask yourself
what you can learn today.

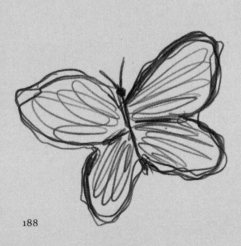

THE LIGHT
THROUGH YOUR STORY
HAS THE ABILITY
TO BE A LAMPPOST
ON SOMEONE'S
JOURNEY.

NOW IS THE TIME
TO BE PRESENT
TO THOSE
WHO ARE WHERE
YOU USED TO BE.
AND THERE
MIGHT NOT
EVEN BE A NEED
TO GIVE ADVICE...

WHILE I MAY FEEL THAT I DON'T MATTER, I AM PART OF GENERATIONS OF GENEROUS HEARTS WHO GAVE THEIR ALL TO MAKE SOMETHING BETTER FOR THOSE WHO CAME AFTER THEM. GOODNESS RUNS THROUGH OUR VEINS. IT UNDERSCORES OUR FAMILY NAME. AND I'M A PART OF THAT.

Dewdrops drip from her wings,
and sunlight dances on the rouge of her skin.

But all she remembers is the creature
with spots and blotches,
whose slimy legs once squirmed along a branch,

embarrassed by how her appearance
is unsmooth in contrast
to other creatures she has observed.

She hides away in a cocoon,
and in that cocoon,
in that place
where she felt forced
to sit with herself,

she learned to love herself
and found the confidence
to unveil wings.

And now
she dances
among the roses,
free to flit and fly and go.
They call her beautiful
and charming,

but what she knows
is that she was filled
with beauty even before
she was fully transformed
into who she has become.

Home is not just a place.
Home is where you know
you are safe
to be still for a while
and simply live.
Simply be.

So if you are longing
for the slow, steadiness of home,
you will find it
by learning to slow your search
of trying to find a particular place
and embrace right here where you are in this body.
You are learning to be within this frame,
with deeply rooted gratitude.

You are learning that it is more
than enough to spend forever
dwelling in the Light that has found you.

And through Light you are able to know "home"
in an all-new heart-opening way.
You are able to look forward
to a future you don't yet know
and still be okay.

THE FUTURE HOLDS A PROMISE OF SOMETHING BEAUTIFUL WORTH KNOWING.

Even as you come back home, continue the good work. Continue being curious. Continue being present with love. Continue resting, for this world needs more rested people. Continue discovering what interests you. You haven't seen all there is to see, and that's a glorious thing. Dare to trust, you are only just beginning.

As you begin to move onward,
you will have to look back,
and when you look back and find
millions of moments
that you have lived through,
you will get to decide
what you pay attention to.

You can decide to soak
in bitterness or wisdom,
resentment or contentment.
The choice is up to you.
The colors you imbue
flying forward
will depend upon what you choose.

5 SIGNS THINGS ARE COMING FULL CIRCLE IN YOUR LIFE

1
When you visit old places, old ideas, or old ways of thinking, you are more aware of how these things make you feel.

2
You are no longer unkind to yourself when the past bubbles up. You know that you have learned from who you were, and there is grace to carry on.

3
You are recognizing that what you have been through can help others. Not that you have all the advice they will ever need, but your story is a gift to others who are longing to be seen and understood on this journey.

4
You have gratitude for how far you have come, knowing that as long as you are living there is more ahead of you that is worth holding out for and looking forward to.

5
You have more patience for those who disagree with you or who may not have had the life experiences you have had.

There is more to our story,
not because we have everything right
or because the future
always seems bright,
but because by waking up
each new day,
we bask in the Light
and have the audacity
to stay in pursuit
of life where others can live
in the grace-lined truth:
"I do know where you have been,
and I do know there is more to you."
And we are only just beginning.

ABOUT THE AUTHOR

Popular poet and artist Morgan Harper Nichols (@morganharpernichols) has garnered a loyal online following of over two million, and the poetry and art she shares is created in response to the personal stories submitted by her community. Morgan and her husband, Patrick, are the proud parents of their son, Jacob, and together, they created Garden24, an online shop featuring Morgan's art. In 2021, Morgan was diagnosed with autism and is passionate about being a part of projects that help others receive support and encounter grace right where they are. She and her family live in Atlanta, Georgia.

IF YOU ENJOYED THIS BOOK, YOU MAY LIKE THESE OTHER BOOKS BY MORGAN HARPER NICHOLS

All Along You Were Blooming is a dynamic collection of illustrated poetry and prose inspiring you to live boundlessly right where you are.

In *How Far You Have Come*, Morgan Harper Nichols encourages you to reclaim moments of brokenness, division, and pain and re-envision them as experiences of reconciliation, unity, and hope.